AF504823

DRAWING NEAR TO GOD

A Study for Teen Girls

Draw near to God and He will draw near to you. James 4:8a

Cynthia Lanius

Drawing Near to God: A Study For Teen Girls

ISBN 979-8-9880304-1-6

Copyright © 2023 by Cynthia Lanius. All rights reserved.
Drawing Near to God: A Study For Teen Girls is the private property of Cynthia Lanius. No part of this publication may be used, reproduced, or transmitted in any form or by any means without written permission from the author, except for brief quotations.

Scripture quotations are often taken from the (NASB®) New American Standard Bible®, Copyright © 1995 by The Lockman Foundation. Used by permission. All rights reserved. www.lockman.org

Printed in the United States of America

❧ Table of Contents ❧

❧ Dedication ❧

This book is dedicated to:

- The young ladies of the Creekview church of Christ – Anna, Kinley, and Layla – who motivated the publication of this book. They are a joy and a blessing.

- To those at the Overland church in Lawrenceburg, Kentucky that originally inspired its writing. Thank you for asking me to teach. What a blessing that was.

- And to all the young girls and women that I've known throughout the years who helped me to see Christ in them.

❧ DIRECTIONS ❧

FOR STUDENTS:

- Prepare "Class Preparation" pages ahead of class, following all directions. (Sometimes it may include other pages. If so, they will be specified.)
- Otherwise, "Class Readings" before class are optional unless otherwise specified by your teacher..

FOR THE TEACHER:

All materials are designed to motivate class discussions. One suggestion is to have the students use a highlighter to highlight what they consider to be important thoughts as they read the "Class Readings" together. Then these can be used at the end of the study to review each lesson. Activity sheets that can be used in any lesson are at the end of the book.

Sample of God's attributes list from question one of all lessons:

Student Name	Bible Verse	Attribute

❧ LESSON 1 ❧

DRAW NEAR TO GOD
Class Preparation

◊ **Things to Do:**

I.   Write a passage that gives an attribute or description of God. We will create a class list throughout the quarter. (Hint: You will find many in Psalms.)

II.   Read James 4:8a.
A. What is God's promise to us in this verse?

B. What is the condition upon which the promise is based?

III.   Read Hebrews 10:22.
With what kind of heart should we draw near to God?

IV.   Read Isaiah 59:1-2
What separates us from God?

V.   Read Ephesians 3:14-20.
A. In Paul's prayer for the Ephesians, name one spiritual blessing that he asked for them? (vs. 14-19)

B. What does Paul say God is able to do? How does He do it? (vs. 20)

C. What is due God? (vs. 21)

Question for Class Discussion: In James 4:8, God offers us a standing invitation to an intimate love relationship with Him—a relationship that makes our lives the best that we can be. But we must open our hearts up to God, what He calls, "Draw near." Jesus promised "rest" to all who would come to Him. Read Matthew 11:28: "Come to me, all you who are weary and burdened, and I will give you rest." How do young people become "weary and burdened" today? Can Jesus give them "rest" from those things? Is Jesus the answer to the problems of today's youth?

❧ LESSON 1 ❧
DRAW NEAR TO GOD
Class Reading

Just think of it, in this study we are going to learn about God, think about Him, read of Him, talk of Him, praise Him, meditate on His character, and reflect on what he wants for us and from us. What a great honor it is to know God. Knowing God can be our strongest motivation to serve Him and to submit to Him. We are focusing on the *person* that God is, to increase our desire to please Him.

Maybe we don't emphasize God's nature enough in our teaching and preaching. We will talk a lot in this study about King David because He is an example to us of someone who was near to God. "I love You, O LORD, my strength. The LORD is my rock and my fortress and my deliverer, My God, my rock, in whom I take refuge; My shield and the horn of my salvation, my stronghold.³ I call upon the LORD, who is worthy to be praised, And I am saved from my enemies" (Psalms 18:1-3). I want to be close to God the way that David was.

We read about drawing near to God in James 4. ⁸ Draw near to God and He will draw near to you (James 4:8a). This is a promise from God, but it is a conditional promise. God wants us near Him, but He will not draw near to us until we draw near to *HIM*.

If we aren't near to God, then we must be far away. What makes us far from God? "Behold, the Lord's hand is not shortened, that it cannot save, or his ear dull, that it cannot hear; **but your iniquities have made a separation between you and your God**, and your sins have hidden his face from you so that he does not hear (Isaiah 59:1-2). So, it is our sin that separates us from God. We cannot be near to God if we are devoted to sin. This scripture says it isn't that God *couldn't* save us. His hand wasn't too short, nor had

He lost his hearing. But *they* were the problem. Their sin was the problem.

Jesus told some Pharisees and teachers of the law "You hypocrites! Isaiah was right when he prophesied about you: 'These people honor me with their lips, but their hearts are far from me'" (Matthew 15:7-8). Our heart can separate us from God. Perhaps we are just negligent, too busy with other things to think much about God.

Imagine a dirty beggar being invited to the White House to sit at a sumptuous feast with the president. The president takes him and washes him and clothes him in beautiful clothes. He even adopts him as his very own child. This is inconceivable, but we are that beggar, invited by God into His kingdom. He washes us by the blood of Jesus, clothes us with His righteousness, and adopts us as His children (1 Corinthians 6:11; Galatians 4:4-6). Let us thank God for His great invitation.

❧ LESSON 1 ❧

DRAW NEAR TO GOD
Class Reading: Our Glorious God

We sing so often of the glory of God, and yet, it is not often that we try to understand what it is that we are singing about. The English word "glory" occurs 402 times in the KJV, so let us see what we can learn about this important quality of God. Even then, we will just touch the hem of the garment of the topic.

The English word glory means magnificence or great beauty. The glory of God is like a diamond with many dazzling facets. Imagine holding a diamond up to the light and seeing its beauty. That is a tiny taste of witnessing the glory, the beauty, the light of God.

"The heavens are telling of the glory of God; And their expanse is declaring the work of His hands. ²Day to day pours forth speech, And night to night reveals knowledge" (Psalm 19:1-2). What are the heavens saying? They are telling us of the glory of God. We see it every day—the glory of His creation. To God be the glory. Great things He hath done. Just look around at creation. It is glorious, just beautiful. Open your eyes. The Lord is like this, only better.

John 1:14 says, "And the Word became flesh, and dwelt among us, and we saw His glory, glory as of the only begotten from the Father, full of grace and truth." His grace and truth are beautiful! They are glorious!

Many times, God's glory is described as something to be seen. The passage above in John says, "We saw His glory." Open your "eyes" and see the beauty of the Lord. "Seeing" it is recognizing it, appreciating it, and valuing it. Our God is glorious (beautiful) in His holiness, in His uniqueness, and in everything that He is. Look at all the characteristics that we will study about God. Just look and see! He is beautiful! He is glorious!

We have a responsibility to give glory to God. It is said of Abraham, "Yet, with respect to the promise of God, he did not waver in unbelief but grew strong in faith, giving glory to God" (Romans 4:20). Psalm 86:12 says, "I will give thanks to You, O Lord my God, with all my heart, And will glorify Your name forever."

Jesus said, "Let your light so shine before men, that they may see your good works, and glorify your Father which is in heaven" (Matthew 5:16). The moon does not generate light on its own, but reflects the light of the sun. Jesus is our light source. Like the moon reflects the light of the sun, we reflect the light of Jesus as we live for Him. Opportunities to shine surround us each day. But careful because we can also tarnish the glory of God if we mistreat others.

✍ LESSON 2 ✍
BELIEVE THAT HE IS
Class Preparation

◊ **Things to Do:**

I. Write a passage that gives an attribute or description of God.

II. Read Hebrews 11:6.
What are the two things listed in this verse required to come to God?

III. Read Joshua 2.
A. Who in this chapter demonstrates great belief in God?

B. How was her belief obtained (vs 10-11)?

C. How did she demonstrate her faith?

IV. Choose another bible character that is an example of great faith (If you need a hint, look in Hebrews 11). How did the person demonstrate faith?

V.   Read: James 2:20-24.
        Describe faith without works.

VI.   Read: Rom 10:17.
        How do *we* obtain faith?

Question for Class Discussion: Is our belief strong? Is it strong enough to bend our will to God's? Is it strong enough to give up selfishness and pride? Is it strong enough to give us joy? Let us reflect on our belief and how it impacts our lives. Read Hebrews 11, 1 John 5:5, and James 2:20.

Who said this???

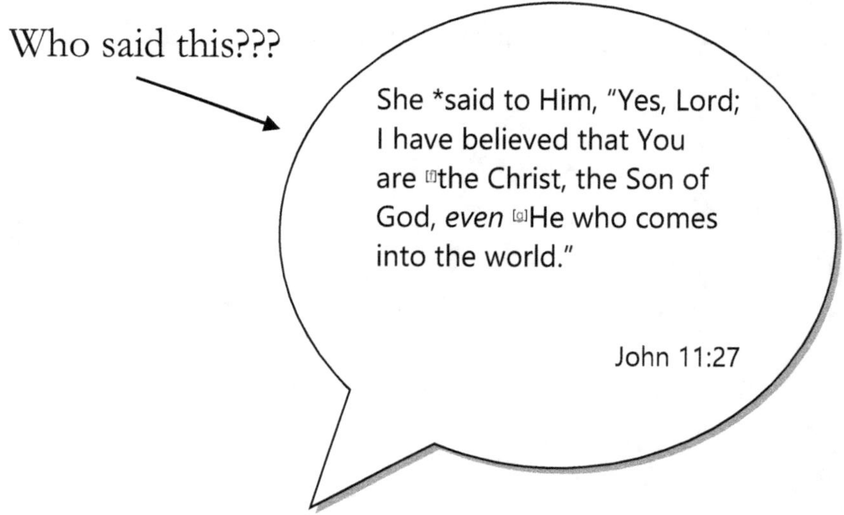

"… for he who comes to God **must believe that He is**
and *that* He is a rewarder of those who seek Him" (Hebrews 11:6b).
According to this passage, two things are required to come to God.
In this lesson we will focus on the first of those requirements –
believing that He is. Our faith is the underpinning of all our service
to God. We may tend to minimize our need for strengthening our
faith and move on to things that we think are greater challenges, but
it is our faith and trust in God that will cause us to seek Him. By
faith, Abraham, Moses, Daniel, and all the other great faithful of
old, obeyed, sometimes, in very difficult circumstances.

One way we can build our faith in God is by observing His
creation. The complexity of the universe demands a designer who
created the "heavens and the earth." Imagine a box of Legos being
tossed out at random on a table. Then imagine them coming
together by themselves to form the picture on the box. That is
more credible than the universe being formed without a designer
and creator.

Nehemiah 9:6 – "You alone are the Lord; You have made
heaven, the heaven of heavens, with all their host, the earth and
everything on it." Psalm 86:8-10 – "He alone is God. There is none
like Him among the gods. All nations should worship Him, because
he made them."

A second way to build belief is by examining His word. It is
faultless even though it was written down by over 40 different
authors from all walks of life: shepherds, farmers, tentmakers,
physicians, fishermen, priests, philosophers, and kings over a period

of some 1,500 years, from around 1450 B.C. (the time of Moses) to about 100 A.D. (following the death and resurrection of Jesus Christ). Examine the prophecies that were fulfilled by Jesus hundreds of years after they were uttered. Has any book held the importance throughout history that this book has?

A third way to build faith is to look at the faith of others, in particular, the great heroes of old that we read about in the scriptures. Why was Daniel willing to pray under threat of death? Or the young man David to battle the giant soldier Goliath? Or the disciples of Jesus to suffer the many persecutions even unto death? Were the hundreds or even thousands delusional, or was it rational choice?

God has given us sufficient evidence to believe that He is. Consequently, we make the choice to believe or disbelieve. If we say there is no God, we think we have no responsibility to Him. If we say that there is One who created us and sustains us and expects something from us, then that brings responsibilities. It requires not only to believe in God, but also to *believe* God. When God says something, we must believe it and follow it.

We know that we must believe that Jesus is our Savior, the Son of God to become a follower of Him, but this is only the beginning of our relationship with God. Jesus said, "He that believes and is baptized shall be saved" (Mark 16:16). If you have not begun your life with Christ as His follower, you can do that today. It will be the best decision that you ever make and will change your life forever.

❧LESSON 2❧
BELIEVE THAT HE IS
Class Reading WHAT WE BELIEVE ABOUT HIS DEITY

Belief in Jesus as deity, as the Son of God, is fundamental to our salvation. Jesus said in John 8:24, "Therefore I said to you that you will die in your sins; for unless you believe that I am He, you will die in your sins." In Mark 16:16, He told his apostles, "He who has believed and has been baptized shall be saved; but he who has disbelieved shall be condemned."

The apostle Thomas refused to believe that Jesus had risen saying that he would not believe if he did not see the nail scars. After seeing Jesus, Thomas declared "My Lord and my God," Jesus said to him, "Because you have seen Me, you have believed. Blessed *are* those who have not seen and *yet* have believed." John then records: "Therefore many other signs Jesus also performed in the presence of the disciples, which are not written in this book; [31] but these have been written so that you may believe that Jesus is the Christ, the Son of God; and that believing you may have life in His name" (John 20:29-31). That is how we learn to believe.

Think of all that our belief in Jesus as the Son of God entails. We believe that Jesus is God, having every characteristic of God (Hebrews 1:3). We believe His every word is true and His every act is righteous and just. That His love is as the Father's love. Believing in Jesus means that we will submit our lives in devotion to Him as Lord and Master.

The apostle Peter, who had closely walked and talked with Jesus, wrote, "And though you have not seen Him, you love Him, and though you do not see Him now, but believe in Him, you greatly rejoice with joy inexpressible and full of glory, [9] obtaining as the outcome of your faith the salvation of your souls" (1 Peter 1:8-9). That is how we believe in Jesus. We "rejoice with joy inexpressible and full of glory" because of our salvation which is the outcome of our faith.

Believing in Jesus as the Christ, the Son of God, is not a one-time act. We cannot say, "Now I believe, so I can check that off the list." We continually grow our faith by the Word of God. The Holy Spirit revealed to Christians, "But grow in the grace and knowledge of our Lord and Savior Jesus Christ" (2 Peter 3:18)

❧ LESSON 3 ❧

SEEK HIM
Class Preparation

◊ **Things to Do:**

I.   Write a passage that gives an attribute or description of God.

II.   Read Deuteronomy 4:29.
This passage says to the children of Israel that they will find God if they do what?

III.   Read Psalms 63:1

    A. How did David seek (watch for) God?

    B. Describe the metaphor that David used to illustrate his seeking.

IV.   Read 2 Chronicles 12:14.
This passage says that Rehoboam did evil because?

V.   Read the story starting on the next page about King Asa and answer these true/false questions.

____________1. Asa sought the Lord all his life.

____________2. Asa's righteous deeds as a young king pleased God

____________3. Zerah, the Ethiopian, led an army of one million men and three hundred chariots into Judah.

____________4. Asa sought God's help to save Judah from Zerah's army.

____________5. God refused to help and Judah fell.

____________6. When Judah and Asa entered into a covenant to seek the LORD, with all their heart and soul, they experienced more than 20 years of peace and prosperity.

____________7. When the Northern Kingdom wanted to come against them, Asa sought God's help again.

____________8. It pleased God for Asa to use his own initiative.

____________9. Asa's refusal to seek God caused his leadership to deteriorate.

____________10 We seek God's will for us today through His word.

A Biblical Example: Asa

Asa was a descendant of David and the third king of the southern kingdom of Judah. He ruled for forty-one years (1 Kings 15:10) and "did what was good and right in the eyes of the Lord his God" (2 Chronicles 14:2). The biblical account of Asa's reign is detailed in 1 Kings 15 and 2 Chronicles 14–16. Asa **commanded the land of Judah to seek the LORD** and to obey His laws and commands. He removed the high places and incense altars in every town in Judah (**2 Chronicles 14:2-5).**

These righteous deeds pleased God and as a consequence the nation enjoyed peace for ten years **(verses 1, 6).** But after this period of tranquility King Asa faced one of his most challenging tests. Zerah, the Ethiopian, led an immense army of one million men and three hundred chariots into Judah **(verse 9).** Asa cried out to God imploring Him for help. Asa called to the LORD his God and said, "LORD, there is no one like you to help the powerless against the mighty. Help us, O LORD our God, for we rely on you, and in your name we have come against this vast army. O LORD, you are our God; do not let man prevail against you" **(verse 11).** The young king Asa trusted in God and His power. As a result, God gave Judah a mighty victory **(verse 13)** along with a huge amount of plunder from cities all around their victory. So what appeared to be a potential disaster turned out to be a source of great prosperity.

After the battle, God sent His prophet Azariah to meet the victorious King to deliver an important message. The prophet said, "The LORD is with you while you are with Him. **If you seek Him, He will be found by you**; but if you forsake Him He will forsake you" **(2 Chronicles 15:2).** The people responded with enthusiasm and confirmed their desire to follow the good example of their king. In **Chapter 15:10-12**, we read: They assembled at Jerusalem in the third month of the fifteenth year of Asa's reign. At that time they sacrificed to the LORD seven hundred head of cattle and seven thousand sheep and goats from the plunder they had brought back. **They entered into a covenant to seek the LORD, the God of their fathers, with all their heart and soul.** Judah and Asa then experienced more than 20 years of peace and prosperity.

But war threatened them again in the 36th year of Asa's reign. This time it was the northern kingdom of Israel that came against them. Rather than seeking God's help, Asa worked out his own plan. He took the silver and gold out of the treasuries of the

LORD'S temple and of his own palace and sent it to Ben-Hadad king of Aram, who was ruling in Damascus. "Let there be a treaty between me and you," he said, "as there was between my father and your father. See, I am sending you silver and gold. Now break your treaty with Baasha king of Israel so he will withdraw from me" **(16:2-3).**

Asa's plan seemed to work. Ben Hadad went to war against the northern kingdom who ceased threatening Judah, but God was not pleased. Hanani the seer came to Asa king of Judah and said to him: "Because you relied on the king of Aram and not on the LORD your God, the army of the king of Aram has escaped from your hand. Were not the Cushites and Libyans a mighty army with great numbers of chariots and horsemen? Yet when you relied on the LORD, he delivered them into your hand. For the eyes of the LORD range throughout the earth to strengthen those whose hearts are fully committed to him. You have done a foolish thing, and from now on you will be at war" **(16:7-9).**

Asa was so enraged with the seer that he put him in prison and brutally oppressed some of the people **(16:10)**. Asa's disobedience caused his leadership to deteriorate. A once outstanding king becomes a great oppressor of the people because of his disobedience and pride. Sadly, Asa set himself on a course of judgment and an early death. In the thirty-ninth year of his reign, Asa was afflicted with a disease in his feet. Though his disease was severe, even in his illness he did not seek help from the LORD, but only from the physicians. Then in the forty-first year of his reign Asa died and rested with his fathers **(16:12-13**).

So, a story that began so wonderfully ends in tragedy. A young leader who relied fully on the Lord ceased to seek Him. Remember his words as he sought God before he went to the early battle: "Help us, O LORD our God, for we rely on you." Let those be our words forever. We can know His will for us today through the word. We must seek it and follow it. This is the way that we rely on God today.

❧ LESSON 3 ❧
SEEK HIM
Class Reading

In the last lesson we focused on the first of the requirements to come to God – believe that He is. In this lesson we focus on the second—believe that He rewards those who seek Him. I believe the reward is that we will find Him, similar to the promise in Deuteronomy 4:29. Do we believe this promise-- that if we seek him with our whole heart, we will find Him?

Think of the things that we seek. When a child is missing, the nation is alerted through an Amber Alert so that as many as possible can seek the missing child. If it were one of our own, imagine how diligently we would seek him. What else, if you lost it today, would you seek frantically? How we seek what we treasure!

We also seek goals. Perhaps we set a goal to become a runner or to get a college degree or maybe to play a musical instrument. We diligently seek to attain these goals. Or perhaps we lose interest and give up. How many resolutions we make, but don't keep.

Understanding our seeking of these physical things can help us to understand how we need to seek God. If we are not diligently seeking God, we are diligently seeking self. We are living our lives for self. Oh, we may be members of the church. We may go to every service. But are we yearning for God? Do our hearts reach out to Him constantly? If we do not yearn for Him, then we need to examine our hearts – to set our hearts – as we will see in our study.

As we do our study of seeking God, you may be surprised how many scriptures contain the concept. Start with a concordance or a searchable bible to find all the references. Examine each one. Study the context of who is saying it, to whom it is being said, and why. Write these things down. Make notes of anything that it makes you think of or wonder about.

If you find at the end of the day that you've been too busy to seek God, then you've been too busy. Our day is not over until we've sought God. "Every day without God is a bad day." Even if you are tired, gather your bible and study for at least 15 minutes before you go to sleep. Then pray to God to praise Him and examine your day with Him. You'll be glad you did! Please don't say, I'll catch up tomorrow unless there is an extreme emergency. Nothing can make our lives richer than studying the word EVERY day. If you get in this habit now, your life will be blessed. This is seeking Him, and if we do it with our whole hearts, he has promised that we will find Him.

☙ LESSON 4 ❧

LOVE GOD
WITH YOUR WHOLE HEART
Class Preparation

◊ **Things to Do:**

I. Write a passage that gives an attribute or description of God.

II. Read Matthew 22:37.

Thought question: Was it important to God that people in Old Testament times loved Him? How would you conclude this from this passage?

III. Give an example of someone from the scriptures that you would say loved the Lord whole-heartedly. How do you know?

IV. Read Romans 5:8 and 1 John 4:19.

A. How did God demonstrate His love for us?

B. From I John 4:19, why do we love God?

C. Name one way we can demonstrate our love for God.

V. Remember the song *God is so Good* (by Paul Makai)?

> God is so good, [sing three times],
> He's so good to me.
>
> He saves my soul, [sing three times],
> and He makes me whole.
>
> I praise His name, [sing three times],
> He's so good to me.

Let's try writing words to another verse.
(Four syllables), [sing three times], (Five syllables).
We will work together on this in class. For now, just give it a try.

Question for Class Discussion: 1 John 4:19 says, "We love Him because he first loved us." Describe some of the ways that God shows His love for us. How do our hearts respond to that love from God?

∞LESSON 4∞
LOVE GOD
WITH YOUR WHOLE HEART
Class Reading

We read in Matthew 22 of a question posed by a Pharisee to Jesus, testing him. [6] "Teacher, which is the great commandment in the Law?" Jesus answered in verse 37, And He said to him, "'YOU SHALL LOVE THE LORD YOUR GOD WITH ALL YOUR HEART, AND WITH ALL YOUR SOUL, AND WITH ALL YOUR MIND.' [38] This is the great and [a]foremost commandment. "Loving God with our whole being. Why would we love God so much? 1 John 4:19 says, "We love Him because he first loved us."

God's love motivates a reciprocal love for Him. He expressed His love in the sacrifice of His Son. So, the answer to these questions is we love Him because of what He has done for us. Do we doubt His great love considering His great gift? Does it not deserve our own whole-hearted love? When I think of what loving God means, I think of small children. They sometimes color a picture and bring it to their mother with love as a gift. Or maybe they pick a dandelion and bring it to mommy. Think of it, what could a tiny child give to their parents? Everything that they have comes from their parents. But this gift of love, as "worthless" as it is in silver or gold, brings joy to the parent's heart. It must be similar to our gifts that we give to God, our gifts of service. We have nothing of material value that we could give God that He needs. But I imagine Him accepting the gifts of our service in the same way as a mother accepts the gifts from her children.

Our love for God is 1. An emotion 2. An action and 3. A commitment.

"

1. The **emotion** of love is our heart and mind recognizing His character and worshipping Him because of it. It is the awesome wonder that we experience when we consider all the worlds His hands have made. It is how we scarcely can take it in when we think that He did not spare his Son but sent Him to die. Those ideas from that great song "How Great Thou Art" express the emotion of love. Think of how many examples we have of David's love for God through worship. How wonderful it is to think of God every day, to worship Him privately in our hearts and to share with others. This is why we are studying His attributes, to know and love Him more and more.

2. The **action** of love for God is obedience, avoiding sin because of our love for Him. Later we will study a lesson on loving God by obeying Him.

3. The **commitment** of love towards God is perseverance, never giving up on our relationship with Him. Because we love God, we will not give up our relationship. The apostle Paul is a great example of commitment. Think of all he went through. 2 Corinthians 4:8 "We are hard pressed on every side, but not crushed; perplexed, but not in despair; [9] persecuted, but not abandoned; struck down, but not destroyed." He didn't let persecution crush him. He didn't let it send him into despair. He was persecuted, but not abandoned by God. And even though he was struck down, he didn't let it destroy him. He did not forsake His God and neither can we. It is our commitment of love.

❧ LESSON 4 ❧

LOVE GOD
WITH YOUR WHOLE HEART
Class Reading The Lord Is Good to Us

Even though the English word "providence" is not found in the scriptures, the concept certainly is. God's providence is defined as "the protective care of God." Notice that "provide" is contained in the word providence. God provides for us all. James 1:17 states, "Every good thing given and every perfect gift is from above, coming down from the Father of lights, with whom there is no variation or shifting shadow." God is so good to us.

God's providence is not a magic force field around us that keeps all good in and all bad out. Neither is God a genie granting all our wishes. Think of the apostle Paul praying three times for a "thorn in the flesh" to be removed. God's answer is recorded in 2 Corinthians 12:9: "My grace is sufficient for you, for power is perfected in weakness." God may not take away the source of despair but will give peace and strength to overcome it. Can we pray, "Thy grace is sufficient"? We will be stronger if we do.

Remember when Isaac asked Abraham where the sacrifice was when on their way to offer Isaac? And do you remember Abraham's answer in Genesis 22:8? "Abraham said, 'God will provide for Himself the lamb for the burnt offering, my son.'" Then verse 14 says, "Abraham called the name of that place The LORD Will Provide, as it is said to this day, 'In the mount of the LORD it will be provided.'" Oh, what great significance! The Lord provided a sacrifice in place of Isaac. And the Lord provides a sacrifice in place of us.

Now let us read 1 John 4:19 We love because He first loved us. We love God because of His great love for us. He loved us even when we were sinners rejecting Him. Let us thank God and love Him with all our being.

LESSON 4

LOVE GOD
WITH YOUR WHOLE HEART
LOVE VERSES

⅋Lesson 5⅋

Love God
by Loving Others
Class Preparation

◊ Things to Do:

I.   Write a passage that tells us an attribute of God.

II.   Read I John 4: 7-12.

    A.   If we do not love, then ______________________

    ____________________________________.

    B.   Give two reasons we should love one another (vs. 11-12).

III.   Make a list of relationships that you have (grandparent, parent, etc.). Are there any of these relationships excluded from the command to love?

IV.   Read Ephesians 4:32. What are three things that we are told to do in this verse?

V.   Write three specific ways that you can think of to show love to others.

Question for Class Discussion: Paul describes the elements of love: Love is patient, love is kind. It does not envy, it does not boast, it is not proud. [5] It does not dishonor others, it is not self-seeking, it is not easily angered, it keeps no record of wrongs. [6] Love does not delight in evil but rejoices with the truth. [7] It always protects, always trusts, always hopes, always perseveres. (I Corinthians 13: 4-7). Are these ever hard?   How can we improve where we need to?

❧ LESSON 5 ❧

LOVE GOD
BY LOVING OTHERS
Class Reading

When someone asked Jesus what the most important part of the Law of Moses was, He said, 'You shall love the Lord your God with all your heart, with all your soul, and with all your mind.' This is the first and great commandment. And the second is like it: 'You shall love your neighbor as yourself.' On these two commandments hang all the Law and the Prophets" (Matthew 22:37-40). God is love. He has done so much for us that we want to return that love, but how?

One very important way is to love others. In fact, Jesus says that when we serve others, we serve Him, and when we fail to serve others, we fail to serve Him (Matthew 25:31-46). In this scene, the people ask, when did we see you hungry? It is as if they are saying, oh Jesus, we would have served *you*, Jesus. If *you'd* been there, Jesus, we'd have served *you*. But Jesus is pointing out that how we serve Him is by serving others, and not just others, but the *least* of others. The least of others may be an older lady in the congregation in a nursing home. The least of others may be someone who annoys us, but needs our love. The least of others may be a brother or sister, or even a parent who is having a hard day. We all have the least of others in our lives that Jesus expects us to love if we love Him.

Can we focus every day on loving God by loving others. We want to do a small kindly deed for others every day. Not just for this week but for a lifetime. Remember, acts become habits. Habits become character. Offer your "cup of cold water" to someone in the name of God. Remember this song?

Just a cup of cold water in His name given, may the hope in some heart renew; do not wait to be told, nor by sorrow driven to the work God has planned for you.

Wake up every day saying, who can I serve today? Can I say a kind word to someone at school? Who needs my help today? Serve God by serving others. Love God by loving others.

LESSON 5

LOVE GOD
BY LOVING OTHERS
Class Reading

Who needs me today? What can I do to help others today? It doesn't have to be a big, huge deal. It may just be a smile and a hello to older ladies in the congregation. Every Sunday morning, just say, I am going to smile and say hello to a widow lady today. It could be a card or a hug to someone you know that needs encouragement. Tell someone how much you appreciate them. Thank your parents for their care of you. But whatever it is, we need to learn to cultivate a daily habit of service.

In the same way that we looked at love for God as emotion, action, and commitment, our love for others can be thought of in these same three ways.

The **emotion of love** for others is expressed in Ephesians 4:31-32. Paul instructs us to "Let all bitterness, and wrath, and anger, and clamour, and evil speaking, be put away from you, with all malice: And be ye kind one to another, tenderhearted, forgiving one another, even as God for Christ's sake hath forgiven you." It is not good for us to hold onto anger and resentment. Being kind and compassionate means doing whatever is beneficial and benevolent to others. Forgiving one another is extending grace, treating others as Christ treats us. This is not always easy, but if we pray to God for help, we can overcome these heart issues.

Actions of Love for One Another

The scriptures give us details of how to treat one another with love. We don't have to wonder.

Be devoted to one another (Romans 12:10).
Honor one another above yourselves (Romans 12:10).

Live in harmony with one another (Romans 12:16).
Build up one another (Romans 14:19; 1 Thessalonians 5:11).
Be likeminded towards one another (Romans 15:5).
Accept one another (Romans 15:7).
Admonish one another (Romans 15:14; Colossians 3:16).
Greet one another (Romans 16:16).
Care for one another (1 Corinthians 12:25).
Serve one another (Galatians 5:13).
Bear one another's burdens (Galatians 6:2)
Forgive one another (Ephesians 4:2, 32; Colossians 3:13).
Be patient with one another (Ephesians 4:2; Colossians 3:13)
Speak the truth in love (Ephesians 4:15, 25).
Be kind and compassionate to one another (Ephesians 4:32).
Speak to one another with psalms, hymns and spiritual songs
(Ephesians 5:19).
Submit to one another (Ephesians 5:21, 1 Peter 5:5).
Consider others better than yourselves (Philippians 2:3).
Look to the interests of one another (Philippians 2:4).
Bear with one another (Colossians 3:13).
Teach one another (Colossians 3:16).
Comfort one another (1 Thessalonians 4:18).
Encourage one another (1 Thessalonians 5:11)
Exhort one another (Hebrews 3:13).
Stir up [provoke, stimulate] one another to love and good works
(Hebrews 10:24).
Show hospitality to one another (1 Peter 4:9).
Employ the gifts that God has given us for the benefit of one
another (1 Peter 4:10).
Clothe yourselves with humility towards one another (1 Peter 5:5).
Pray for one another (James 5:16).
Confess your faults to one another (James 5:16).

Such a great treasure trove of advice about how to love one
another! Think of your family, of your friends, of the church, of
your enemies, and let us love God by loving one another.

Love for others as Commitment – Love never fails I
Corinthians 13:8a If we love others, we will not give up on our
relationship with them. Never stop loving others!

∾LESSON 6∾

LOVE GOD
BY OBEYING HIM
Class Preparation

◊ **Things to Do:**

I.   Write a passage that tells us something about God.

II.   Read John 14: 15, 23-24. If I don't obey God, what is the logical conclusion from this passage?

III.   Read Romans 3:23. All people have _________________________.

IV.   Read Romans 12:21. Who is someone in the scriptures that you would say was overcome with evil? Who is someone that you would say overcame evil with good?

V.   Christians help one another avoid sin. Match these resources that help keep us from sin.

_________ Encouraging one another at the assemblies.

_________Confess our faults one to another.

_________Carry others' burdens.

_________Encourage and build each other up

1. James 5:16

2. I Thessalonians 5:11

3. Hebrews 10:24

4. Galatians 6:2

Question for Discussion: How should we feel when we disobey God? Read Psalm 51:17. Psalm 51 is: "A psalm of David. When the prophet Nathan came to him after David had committed adultery with Bathsheba." How does David feel about his sin? What does David mean here by someone with a broken heart? What is a contrite heart? But does God want us to continue to mourn over our sin forever? Read verses 7-9. After we ask God for forgiveness, we should be kind to ourselves and say, God has forgiven me and so will I!

❧ LESSON 6 ❧

LOVE GOD
BY OBEYING HIM
Class Reading

Jesus put it very clearly. "'If you love Me, you will keep My commandments'" (John 14:15). If we do not obey, the logical conclusion is that we do not love Jesus. When we fail to obey, we have to admit that our love failed. It is what Jesus said.

Joseph gives us a wonderful example of obedience when Potiphar's wife tried to get him to sin. In Genesis 39:9b, Joseph asked her, "How then could I do this great evil and sin against God?" Have we ever asked ourselves that question when we are tempted to sin? Do we realize the gravity of disobedience, because as Jesus said, if you love me, you will keep my commands?

In I John 5:3, not only did John stress that keeping God's commands shows our love for God, he said that His commands are not "burdensome." God's will is good for me. It is not a burden, and if I love Jesus, and if I love God, I will strive to obey.

We cannot name one command that is bad for us. God's way is the best way for us to live. We must trust that. When God told Abram to go from his country, his people and his father's household to the land He would show him, Abram did what God told him to do even if he had no idea where God was taking him. (Genesis 12:1). Why did he do that? Because he trusted God.

How can I avoid sin? Jesus told his disciples, "Pray that you may not enter into temptation." How fervently did Jesus pray in the garden? Do we fervently pray when we are tempted to sin?

We are not perfect in our love, and we are not perfect in our obedience. But when we disobey, our hearts must grieve that we have failed in our love. Nothing can help us in this more than reading Psalm 51. Oh how it grieved David that he had failed the Lord, but he knew that God yearned for him to turn back to Him.

I must turn away from sin and back to God. I must pray "Create in me a clean heart, O God, And renew a steadfast spirit within me" (Psalm 51:10). God will restore us. Read Luke 15 and see the joy of the Father to have his rebel son return.

We have probably sung the old hymn Trust and Obey hundreds of times. But do we really consider its words? Look at what it says, "Trust and obey, for there's no other way To be happy in Jesus, but to trust and obey."

'If you love Me, 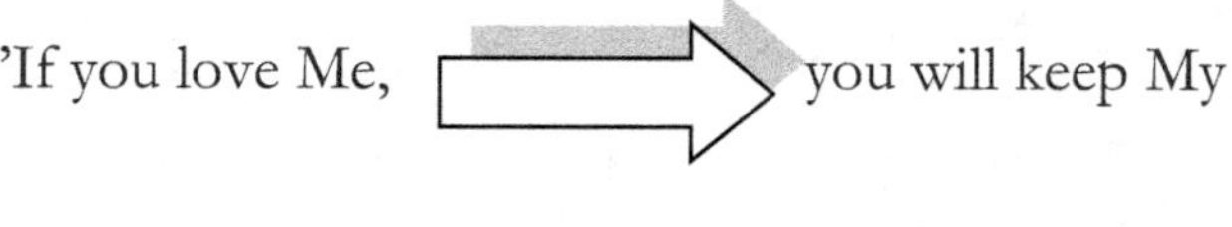 you will keep My

commandments'" (John 14:15).

❦LESSON 6❧

LOVE GOD
BY OBEYING HIM
Class Reading: God the Lawgiver

God is love and His law is an expression of His love. We would not even know love without it. Likewise, God is righteous, and His law is an expression of His righteousness. We cannot be righteous without it. Trying to have a relationship with God without obeying His law is futile.

We know that all the scriptures, both Old and New Testaments, are the inspired word of God and contain God's law. 2 Timothy 3:16-17 says, "All Scripture is inspired by God and profitable for teaching, for reproof, for correction, for training in righteousness; [17]so that the man of God may be adequate, equipped for every good work."

We are bound by the law of Christ today rather than the law of Moses as the Psalmists were, but aren't we glad that we have it "for our instruction" (Romans 15:4)?

David said that he loved the law! If we do not see God's law as the Psalmists saw it, as a delight, then maybe we need to pray as in Psalm 119:18: "Open my eyes that I may behold Wonderful things from your law." We need to thank God for His law. Imagine your life without the law of God. A life without the law would be a life without the Lawgiver.

Psalm 40:8 I delight to do Your will, O my God; Your Law is within my heart.
Psalm 94:12 Blessed is the man whom You chasten, O LORD, And whom You teach out of Your law.
Psalm 105:45 So that they might keep His statutes And observe His laws, Praise the LORD!

❧ LESSON 7 ❧
GOD PROVIDES VICTORY
Class Preparation

◊ **Things to Do:**

   I.   Write a passage that tells us about God.

   II.   Read 2 Timothy 4:16-17.

      A. What challenge was Paul experiencing? How did he withstand it?

      B. When pressure is put on us to do wrong, how can we resist the wrong?

   III.   Read Rom 8:31.
What is the answer to this question.

   IV.   Read 1 John 5:4.
What is the victory that overcomes the world?

   V.   Read Job 1.

      A. How did God describe Job? (verse 8)

B. Satan said Job obeyed God for what reason? (verse 10)

C.   Name some problems God allowed Satan to place upon Job. (verses 13-19)

D.   Did Job sin through all these problems? (verse 22)

Question for Class Discussion: Name three problems that young girls face today (this may not be you personally, but things that you may see others facing). How can we overcome these?

✤ LESSON 7 ✤

GOD PROVIDES VICTORY
Class Reading

At times, even for Christians, life can consist of all kinds of struggles, even tragedy. Depression, illness, loneliness, loss of loved ones are just a few of the personal struggles that we may face. Day by day, it is important that we focus our attention, not only on the avoidance of problems, but on conquering the problems that confront us.

The Bible teaches that those who genuinely believe in God will find in their faith the key to being a conqueror. The apostle John wrote, "For everyone who has been born of God overcomes the world. And this is the victory that has overcome the world — our faith. Who is it that overcomes the world except the one who believes that Jesus is the Son of God?" (1 John 5:4-5). Faith in God gives us victory over life's problems.

Whatever hardships or obstacles we face, God is greater than those obstacles. Jesus assured His disciples: "I have said these things to you, that in me you may have peace. In the world you will have tribulation. But take heart; I have overcome the world" (John 16:33). And John, one of the disciples to whom the Lord spoke these words, later wrote: "Little children, you are from God and have overcome them, for he who is in you is greater than he who is in the world" (1 John 4:4).

There is no hardship that can prevent us from becoming the godly person God wants us to be. That is the victory that we are talking about. There is no hardship that can prevent us from walking on that path close to God. That is the victory.

❧ LESSON 7 ❧

GOD PROVIDES VICTORY
Class Reading Deborah

Deborah was a woman of Old Testament times that shows us how to trust God to give victory over life's problems. We read about her in **Judges 4 and 5.**

Let's set the background. After the Israelite judges Ehud, had died, the people did evil. The Lord then sold them into the hand of Jabin, king of Caanan. Sisera was head of Caanan's army. This army harassed and dominated the nation of Israel for some 20 years. Israel cried out for mercy, and God answered those prayers. (4: 1-3). Then we are introduced to Deborah who was a prophetess, wife, and judge who began leading Israel. (4: 4-5).

Let us look at one great event in Deborah's life. Deborah sent for Barak, an Israelite warrior, and said to him, "The LORD, the God of Israel, commands you: 'Go, take with you ten thousand men of Naphtali and Zebulun and lead them up to Mount Tabor" Then God made a great promise. [7] "I will lead Sisera, the commander of Jabin's army, with his chariots and his troops to the Kishon River and give him into your hands'" (4:6-7).

Barak responded by saying to Deborah, "If you will go with me, I will go; if not I will not go" (Judges 4:8). While this was a weakness in faith for Barak—he lacked complete confidence in God—his request attests to the character of Deborah. We do not know for sure what Barak hoped to gain by Deborah's presence. Did he see the lady judge as such a trusted adviser that he wanted her close by? Or that Deborah's presence might inspire the Israelites to fight more valiantly? Or perhaps some other reason.

Regardless, in the next verse, without hesitation, Deborah agrees to go. Deborah went off with Barak, and just as He had promised, God gave them victory over their enemy.

Let's look at four statements that Deborah made and their application to our lives today.

1. **Deborah's Statement:** <u>The Lord God has commanded</u> (4: 6-7) **Application**: Deborah was guided without reservation by what God commanded and so must we be. John 14:15-31 – 'If ye love me, keep my commandments"

2. **Deborah's Statement:** <u>I will surely go with you</u> (4: 9). **Application**: Think of how much courage it would have taken to agree to go with Barak. Clearly, Deborah's faith gave her this courage and so will ours. Joshua 1:9 --Have not I commanded thee? Be strong and of a good courage; be not afraid, neither be thou dismayed: for the LORD thy God *is* with thee whithersoever you go.

3. **Deborah's Statement:** <u>Up! This is the day that the Lord God has delivered</u> (4: 14). **Application**: Deborah did not delay to go to this great work. Likewise, we must be about our work for the Lord. -- 1 Cor 15: 58 Therefore, my beloved brethren, be steadfast, immovable, always abounding in the work of the Lord, knowing that your toil is not *in* vain in the Lord.

4. **Deborah's Statement:** <u>I will sing praise to the Lord</u> (5:3). **Application**: Deborah gave God praise for the great victory as we must. -- 1 Peter 2:9 But you are a chosen people, a royal priesthood, a holy nation, a people belonging to God, that you may declare the praises of him who called you out of darkness into his wonderful light.

Hear this, you kings! Listen, you rulers! I, even I, will sing to the LORD;   I will praise the LORD, the God of Israel, in song.
(Judges 5:3)

❧ LESSON 7 ❧
GOD PROVIDES VICTORY
Class Reading

As the world departs more and more from God's principles, the more that Christians require courage to oppose sin. When sin is condoned and even promoted, it is harder to resist. Alcohol and drugs, pornography and other sexual sins are rampant in our society. Aggression and violence are everyday occurrences. God is not revered. Sin often surrounds us at our workplace or school.

So how do we avoid sin when we are surrounded by it? Jesus was not cowering in the garden, hiding in fear, when the soldiers came for Him. Rather, He had gone to a quiet place to commune with the source of His courage, put on His armor, and prepare for His battle (Isaiah 42:13). As Jesus did, so we should also do. "Finally, be strong in the Lord and in the strength of His might. [11]Put on the full armor of God, so that you will be able to stand firm against the schemes of the devil. [12] For our struggle is not against flesh and blood, but against the rulers, against the powers, against the world forces of this darkness, against the spiritual forces of wickedness in the heavenly places" (Ephesians 6:10-12).

If we would only realize the source of our courage! Let us look at one of the most famous stories of all time in 1 Samuel 17 – David and Goliath. Every day, Goliath, a massive man, had taunted the army of Israel to accept his fight-to-the-death, winner-takes-all challenge. Every morning when he stepped forward, the men of God shrank back in fear until a young shepherd, David, came, heard the taunts, and took up the challenge, saying to Goliath, "This day the LORD will deliver you up into my hands, and I will strike you down and remove your head from you. And I will give the dead bodies of the army of the Philistines this day to the birds of the sky and the wild beasts of the earth, that all the earth may know that there is a God in Israel, [47]and that all this assembly may know that the Lord does not deliver by sword or by spear; for the battle is the Lord's and He will give you into our hands" (1 Samuel 17:46-47).

So, was this a self-confident young man? No, his confidence lay in God. David saw God as more powerful than the feared Philistine, so he went out to fight, believing that God would give him victory. That faith gave David courage, and that kind of faith can give us courage. Never let any "Goliath" loom larger than God.

There are things in the world that Satan uses to draw us away from God. A few common ones include:

The Media: Young people are challenged very early, beginning with their first exposure to television, movies and the internet. Much of the media is aligned against Christian values, and Americans spend much of their free time, (should we say too much) watching some form of television or on the internet. On TV, no one talks of loving God. No one prays. In TV families, do the children honor and obey their parents? Do wives love and honor and submit to their husbands? Any show that has science is almost always evolution based, sometimes subtle, sometimes obvious. We have to be aware and not let it influence us.

Busy-ness: We are challenged by a busy-ness that keeps us from spending the time that we should on our spiritual lives. People in our culture are so busy that they are often stressed and don't devote their lives to God as they should. When I taught high school, I saw many, many young people who came to school exhausted from lack of sleep. Sometimes children are into so many extracurricular activities that the family spends little time together. We must assess our lives and prioritize God's will for us.

We are challenged by **acquaintances**. We must be careful of the friends that we make. 1 Corinthians 15:33 says, "Do not be deceived: Bad company corrupts good morals." And Proverbs 12:26, "The righteous is a guide to his neighbor, But the way of the wicked leads them astray." If we are honest with ourselves, we can know when someone is influencing us for bad. We must be so careful that we influence them for good, not vice versa. Few people that we meet at school have been raised with the same moral principles that we have. Be careful! No matter how much we may be charmed by a person's personality, if we see them acting in an ungodly manner, we must stay away.

We are challenged by **selfishness** that motivates us to please ourselves rather than God or others. Perhaps nothing can rob us of our walk with God like selfishness. Philippians 2:3-4 says, "Do nothing from rivalry or conceit, but in humility count others more significant than yourselves. Let each of you look not only to his own interests, but also to the interests of others." Many examples of unselfish people appear in God's word. Abram dealt unselfishly with Lot when he gave Lot his choice of land. Joseph provided for his brothers and their children even after all his brothers had done to him. Daniel refused any gifts or rewards from King Belshazzar for his interpretation so that he would not gain from God's inspiration, but that God would receive the glory. Paul writes of the best way to overcome selfishness: "Whatever you do, do all to the glory of God."

We are challenged by **youth culture**. It is sometimes tempting to be attracted to what seems cool and popular, which is fine as long as the activity is pure and wholesome. In his letter to the church in Rome, Paul writes, "And do not be conformed to this world, but be transformed by the renewing of your mind, so that you may prove what the will of God is, that which is good and acceptable and perfect" (Romans 12:2). We must not be enticed by "popularity", by the desire to fit in and be accepted, affecting the way we dress, or talk, or the way we act in general. Sometimes we just have to have the courage to be different from others around us. We live in a culture that is very accepting of sin. In fact, we are told that if we do not condone a wide variety of sins, then we are closed-minded and unloving. Don't believe it!

All of our challenges can be overcome. God loves us and wants us to return back to him when we've been overtaken in a fault. All Christians will continue to struggle with sin throughout our lives; however, we should never be satisfied with our sin. Any sinful act goes directly against God. It can be easy for people to rationalize their sin or to believe their sin does not hurt others, yet this could not be further from the truth. We start with a contrite prayer for forgiveness. God will help us overcome our challenges if we let Him.

> Faith gave David courage, and that kind of faith can give us courage. Never let any "Goliath" loom larger than God.

❧ LESSON 8 ☙

BECOMING A GODLY WOMAN
Class Preparation

◊ Things to Do:

I.   Write a passage that tells us about God.

II. Read Romans 16:1-2.
      A. Who does Paul commend?

      B. What was she to the church at Cenchrea?

      C. What had she done for many and even for Paul?

III.   Read 2 Timothy 1:5, Acts 16:1, and 2 Timothy 3:14–15. What do we learn from these passages about important work of women?

IV.   Choose one woman from the list on the next pages and write a paragraph about her.

Question for Class Discussion: Do you have to wait to be old before you can start seeking God? Make a list of some things that you can do right now. Share and discuss.

❧ LESSON 8 ❧

BECOMING A GODLY WOMAN
Resource: Women in the New Testament

Mary (Matt 1:16, 18-25; 2-11, 13-14, 20-21; Matt 12:46-50; Matt 13:55; Mark 3: 31-35; Mark 6:3; Luke 1:26-56; 2:5-8, 16, 19, 22, 27, 34-35, 43-51; Luke 8: 19-20; John 2:1-5, 12; 6:42; John 19:25-27; Acts 1:14; Gal 4:4)

Daughter of Jarius (Matt 9: 18-19, 23-26; Mark 5: 22-24, 35-43; Luke 8:41, 49-56)

Herodias (Matt. 14: 1-11; Mark 6:17-28; Luke 3:19-20)

Herodias' daughter (Matt 14:6-11; Mark: 6: 22-29; Luke 3:19-20)

Woman who Anointed Jesus (Matt 26: 6-13; Mark 14:3-9; John 12:1-8)

Mary Magdalene (Matt 27:57, 61; Matt 28:1-10; Mark 15: 40-41,47; 16: 1-8, 9-11; Luke 8:2-3; 24: 1-11, 22-24; John 19:25; 20: 1-3, 11-18)

Mary, the mother of James and Joses (also called "The other

The Widow who Gave Two Mites (Mark 12:41-44; Luke 21:1-4)

Elisabeth (Luke 1:5-80)

Anna (Luke 2: 36-38)

Widow of Nain (Luke 7: 11-17)

Sinner who washed Jesus Feet with her hair (Luke 7:36-50)

Certain women who had been healed (Luke 8:2-3)

Martha (Luke 10: 37-42; John 11: 1-6, 17-27, 34-45; 12:2)

Mary of Bethany (Luke 10: 37-42; John 11: 1-5, 17-20, 28-34, 39-45; 12:3-9)

Samaritan Woman at the Well (John 4: 7-42)

Woman Taken in Adultery (John 8:1-11)

Sapphira (Acts 5:1-11)

Tabitha/Dorcus (Acts 9:36-42)

Eunice (2 Tim 1:15; Acts 16:1—the son of a certain woman)

Lois (2 Tim 1:15)

Lydia (Acts 16: 11-15, 40)

Damaris (Acts 17:34)

Priscilla (Acts 18:2-3, 18-20, 24-26; Rom. 16: 3-5; 1 Cor. 16:19; 2 Tim 4:19)

❧ LESSON 8 ❧
BECOMING A GODLY WOMAN
Class Reading Some Characteristics of a Godly Woman
Pro 31:10-31

Verses

10 - Who can find a virtuous wife? For her worth is far above rubies.--*Do we desire to be this kind of treasure?*
11-12 - The heart of her husband safely trusts her; so he will have no lack of gain. She does him good and not evil all the days of her life. -- *He can trust that she will not do him wrong in any way.*

13 She seeks wool and flax, and willingly works with her hands. --*In our modern days, most of us do not do this* **specific** *type of work, but the key phrase here is "willingly works." A godly woman is a hard working woman, not lazy.*

14-15 She is like the merchant ships, she brings her food from afar. She also rises while it is yet night, and provides food for her household, and a portion for her maidservants. —*She goes out and brings food into the household. Once again, she is not lazy because she rises up early to provide food. And we learn that she is wealthy enough to have maidservants. She is a wise woman who is handling her responsibilities well.*

16 She considers a field and buys it; From her earnings she plants a vineyard. — *How wise she was!*
17 She girds herself with strength and strengthens her arms. --*Godly women are strong. "Strengthens her arms" implies that she is able to take care of her responsibilities.*

18-19 She perceives that her merchandise is good, and her lamp does not go out by night. She stretches out her hand to the distaff, and her hand holds the spindle.--*She has good judgment, perceiving that her merchandise is good. "Her lamp does not go out at night" implies that she has prepared well for her family's needs.*

20 She extends her hand to the poor, yes, she reaches out her hands to the needy.--*What a godly woman. As busy as she is, she reaches out to help those in need.*

21-22 She is not afraid of snow for her household; for all her household is clothed with scarlet. She makes tapestry for herself;

her clothing is fine linen and purple.--*Once again, she takes care of her responsibilities well.*

23 Her husband is known in the gates, when he sits among the elders of the land.--*He can confidently take his place among community leaders knowing his household is being looked after well.*

24 She makes linen garments and sells them, and supplies sashes for the merchants.--*This business seems to be something that she controls in addition to running her household.*

25 Strength and honor are her clothing; she shall rejoice in time to come.--*The same way that the scriptures say we put on Christ today, she wore strength and honor. A statement of her character.*

26 She opens her mouth with wisdom, and on her tongue is the law of kindness.--*So not only does she act with wisdom, her speech is also wise and kind.*

27 She watches over the ways of her household, and does not eat the bread of idleness.--*She sees to the needs of her household, again not lazy.*

28-29 Her children rise up and call her blessed; her husband also, and he praises her: many daughters have done well, but you excel them all.--*What a joyous thought. Her husband and children appreciate her for what she does. Her husband praises her!!!*

30-31 Charm is deceitful, and beauty is passing, but a woman who fears the Lord, she shall be praised. Give her of the fruit of her hands and let her own works praise her in the gates.--*Others   praise her. Her husband is in the gates, so it must be satisfying to him to hear the good things that others say about this godly and virtuous woman. The kind of woman we strive to become.*

❮Lesson 9❯

Preparing for a
Godly Marriage
Class Preparation

◊ **Things to Do:**

I.   Write a scripture about God.

II.   Read Ephesians 5:22-24.
    A. What is the command to wives in this passage?

    B. What is it compared to?

III.   Read the Story of Aquilla and Priscilla on the following pages and answer the following.

    1) Why had Aquila and Priscilla left Rome?

    2) Where were they living when they first met Paul?
    ____

    3) How long did Paul stay there?__________________

    4) Where did they go next? ______________________________

5) Who did they teach there?

   ____

6) Name two places where the church met in their home.
   _________________ and _________________.

7) What had they done for
   Paul?____

8) How many times was Aquila mentioned without Priscilla?

   ____

9) Which do the scriptures NOT say that Aquila and Priscilla
   did 1) had a preacher stay in their home 2) taught a preacher
   3) preached in the synagogue 4) had the church meet in
   their home.

Question for Discussion: Discuss the four goals of finding a
husband that you read about in the story. Do you have one to add?

❧ LESSON 9 ❧

PREPARING FOR GODLY MARRIAGE

Example of a Godly Marriage:
The Story of Aquila and Priscilla

Aquila and Priscilla were a couple that we read about all through the letters of Paul. They lived in several cities, but as far as we can see, everywhere they went, they were faithful to the Lord, lived close to Him.

In Rome: When we first meet them, Aquila and Priscilla had left Rome. According to Acts 18:2, the Roman emperor Claudius exiled all Jews from the city of Rome. Aquila, along with his wife Priscilla, fled to Corinth. We do not know for certain whether Priscilla was Jewish or Roman since only the husband Aquila is called a Jew. Some believe she may have been Roman since her name was a common aristocratic Roman name. Regardless, they left *together*. They seemed to be always together. One's name never appears in the scriptures without the other. They even worked together as tentmakers (Acts 18:3). How important it is for a couple to be together; God made marriage to provide companionship.

In Corinth: Paul arrived in Corinth and met Aquila and Priscilla there. He shared not only faith with them, but also their occupation. He began to work and live with them. I'm sure you have friends over to visit sometime. Can you imagine what it would have been like to have the apostle Paul stay in your house? Imagine the wonderful conversations they must have had about the Lord Jesus Christ. I can imagine how faith building that would have been. The Apostle Paul stayed a year and a half in Corinth, teaching the word of God among them (Acts 18:11). Think of it, eighteen months of teaching by the apostle Paul. How Aquila and Priscilla must have grown in their faith!

In Ephesus: Their later actions demonstrate how thoroughly Aquila and Priscilla had learned and applied God's Word. When Paul left Corinth, he went to Ephesus, and they went with him (Acts 18:18). Paul left them there, (v 19) and went on to Antioch (v 22) and several other churches (v 23). Then starting in verse 24, it says, "Meanwhile a Jew named Apollos, a native of Alexandria, came to Ephesus. He was a learned man, with a thorough knowledge of the Scriptures. He had been instructed in the way of the Lord, and he spoke with great fervor and taught about Jesus accurately, though he knew only the baptism of John. He began to speak boldly in the synagogue. But when Priscilla and Aquila heard him, they took him aside and explained to him the way of God more accurately" (Acts 18:24-26). Apollos accepted the truth, and because of this meeting with Aquila and Priscilla, he became an effective servant of God. In the next two verses it says that Apollos went to Achaia and proved "from the Scriptures that Jesus was the Messiah." We will never be powerful preachers, but we can be faithful students and private teachers of the Word like Aquila and Priscilla were. **Make it your goal to someday choose a husband who will want to serve with you as a student and teacher of God's word.**

When Paul returned to Ephesus on his third missionary journey, he remained there teaching for approximately three years (Acts 19). While he was there in Ephesus, he wrote his first letter to the Corinthians saying, "The churches of Asia greet you. Aquila and Prisca greet you heartily in the Lord, with the church that is in their house" (I Cor 16:19). They used their home in Ephesus for a meeting place for the church. This will not be the last time that they used their home for that purpose. **Make it your goal to someday choose a husband who will want to serve with you as a worker in the church.**

While we have church buildings today, there is no substitute for the home as a place to help others. The possibilities for using our homes to serve the Lord are many. For example, young people benefit by adults who open their homes to them for bible classes or recreation. People of all ages are encouraged by a visit in the homes of Christians. What a blessing it is to us when we use our home in the service of God. **Make it your goal to someday choose a husband who will want to use your possessions for God's service.**

In Rome: When Paul left Ephesus, Claudius was dead, and Aquila and Priscilla returned to Rome. Paul wrote his epistle to the Romans from Greece on his third missionary journey, and he said, "Greet Prisca and Aquila, my fellow-workers in Christ Jesus, who for my life risked their own necks, to whom not only do I give thanks, but also all the churches of the Gentiles; Also greet the church that is in their house" (Rom 16:3-5). Churches in New Testament times often met in homes, and once again, the home of Aquila and Priscilla was open for that purpose.

Did you notice what Paul said that Aquila and Priscilla had done for him? "Who for my life risked their own necks, to whom not only do I give thanks…." "Risked their necks" means that they put their own lives in jeopardy to save Paul's. We do not know exactly when or how they did this. Jesus had said, "Greater love has no one than this, that someone lay down his life for his friends." This godly couple was willing to give everything in the service of the Savior, even their lives. Do you believe that they were made stronger because they had the support of one another? Think of how having a godly husband can strengthen. Read Ecclesiastes 4:9-10. **Make it your goal to someday choose a husband who will help you to be strong in the Lord.**

In Ephesus: Aquila and Priscilla are mentioned once more in the New Testament, in the last chapter of the last book the Apostle Paul wrote. It had been about fifteen years since Paul first met them at Corinth, and now he was in a Roman prison. His death at the hands of the emperor Nero was at hand, and these were among his last recorded words before he died. "Greet Prisca and Aquila, and the household of Onesiphorus" (2 Tim 4:19). He was thinking of his dear friends who were then back in Ephesus where Timothy was working, possibly having left Rome to escape Nero's latest persecution against Christians. It was just a brief and simple greeting, using the shorter form of Priscilla's name. But Paul wanted to be remembered to them at the end of his life, demonstrating how much he loved them.

May we all strive to someday be a part of a godly couple that serves the Lord "two-gether."

Map that shows travels of Aquilla and Priscilla.

❧ LESSON 9 ❧
PREPARING FOR GODLY MARRIAGE
Class Reading

With its life-long consequences, choosing who we will marry is the second most important decision we will ever make, second only to choosing to serve God. So how do we decide? Do we just "fall in love" with someone who makes our heart melt? Let us consider some principles from God to help us decide.

I. You should choose carefully who you date.

Dating is the primary way in our culture that young people get to know one another, and even though there is no specific teaching about dating in the scriptures, all principles that *are* taught also apply to dating. The first rule in dating is the first rule in life: our love for God. Staying focused on our love for God will provide a proper perspective. We will not date someone who does not love God. Also, the Bible *does* teach about the need to maintain purity (1 Corinthians 6:13). Purity is a foreign idea to the world, which promotes sexual immorality, but we must enter marriage pure.

II. You should share the same goals for the future:

Most importantly both of you must have God in the center of your life. You must both live to please Him. As a potential wife, does it give you joy to think of him leading your family? "For the husband is the head of the wife even as Christ is the head of the church, his body, and is himself its Savior" (Ephesians 5:23). Does he treat you with love and respect and put your needs before his own?

You must explore together your values. Be careful as you discuss your differences and what you have in common. The greater the differences the greater the potential for future conflict. Amos asks, "Can two walk together, except they be agreed?" (Amos 3:3).

III. Choose someone who is spiritually mature:

A successful marriage is not based on romantic love but on spiritual maturity. This may be a surprising statement but stop and think with me. Consider the fruit of the Spirit in Galatians 5:22-23. The first word on the list is love. This means that the more spiritually mature the prospective husband and wife are, the more sacrificial love will be in the marriage and the greater the likelihood for success. Also, notice the other signs of spiritual maturity in the list. The next two words are joy and peace. Do you want joy and peace in your relationship? Then patience, kindness, goodness, faithfulness, gentleness, self-control. What wonderful attributes of a marriage. Spiritual maturity is the key. A great marriage has God at its center.

This is such a serious subject. When you are considering marriage, it is best to pray and seek guidance from a wise counselor.

A few bible verses about marriage:

Genesis 2:18: Then the LORD God said, "It is not good that the man should be alone; I will make him a helper fit for him."

Colossians 3:18: Wives, submit to your husbands, as is fitting in the Lord. Husbands, love your wives, and do not be harsh with them.

1 Peter 3:7: Likewise, husbands, live with your wives in an understanding way, showing honor to the woman as the weaker vessel, since they are heirs with you of the grace of life, so that your prayers may not be hindered.

Hebrews 13:4: Let marriage be held in honor among all, and let the marriage bed be undefiled, for God will judge the sexually immoral and adulterous.

✌ LESSON 10 ✌
FOLLOWING JESUS
Class Preparation

◊ Things to Do:

   I.   Write a passage that tells us about God.?

   II.   Read 1 Peter 2:21
For what purpose were we called?

   III.   Read 1 Peter 3:18
Christ died to bring us to whom?

   IV.   Read Romans 5:10.
What did the death of Jesus do?

   V.   Read John 8:12
What is the result of following Jesus?

   V.   Read Hebrews 12:1-2.
Who should we look to as we are running our race towards heaven?

VI.   Read Hebrews 12:3.
       What are we not to do?

VII.   Read 1 Peter 1:8.
       Describe the joy that comes from believing in Jesus.

Question for Class Discussion: How hard is it to follow Jesus? Consider Matthew 16:24 where Jesus said to His disciples, "If anyone wishes to come after Me, he must deny himself, and take up his cross and follow Me." Self-denial can be a tremendous challenge, can it not? But we must trust God to provide us with what we need to accomplish it. Jesus also said that His yoke is easy and His burden is light (Matthew 11:30). Compared to the yoke of evil and the burden of sin, Jesus' yoke is light and easy. Since Jesus says it is easy, we must not make it hard and burdensome.

❧ LESSON 10 ❧

FOLLOWING JESUS
Class Reading: Know Him

We can know God and the Lord Jesus Christ: not just know *about* them but *know them*. When Jesus prayed for His disciples before His death, He prayed, "This is eternal life, that they may know You, the only true God, and Jesus Christ whom You have sent" (John 17:3).

The basics of knowing Jesus is recognizing Him as God. John says in John 1:10: "He was in the world, and the world was made through Him, and the world did not know Him." And John the Baptist said of Jesus, "I baptize in water, but among you stands One whom you do not know" (John 1:26).

All through his writings, the apostle John uses "know" to describe our relationship with God. In 1 John 2:3-6, he said, "By this we know that we have come to know Him if we keep His commandments. [4] The one who says, 'I have come to know Him,' and does not keep His commandments, is a liar, and the truth is not in him; [5] but whoever keeps His word, in him the love of God has truly been perfected. By this we know that we are in Him: [6] the one who says he abides in Him ought himself to walk in the same manner as He walked."

John says it here about as plainly as anyone can: our relationship with God is dependent on our obedience. If we do not keep His commandments, we do not know Him. People often get frustrated when the importance of obedience is stressed. But Jesus said that even *His* love of the Father was demonstrated by *His* obedience. "But so that the world may know that I love the Father, I do exactly as the Father commanded Me" (John 14:31). Just as Jesus' love for the Father is demonstrated by obedience, so is ours.

Paul was describing His relationship with God in 2 Timothy 1:12: "For this reason I also suffer these things, but I am not ashamed; for I know whom I have believed and I am convinced that He is able to guard what I have entrusted to Him until that day." It should be our constant goal to know God more. The prophet Hosea said, "So let us know, let us press on to know the LORD" (Hosea 6:3a).

The central theme of Paul's prayer in Ephesians 1 is that they would know God more deeply. "I do not cease making mention of you in my prayers; [17]that the God of our Lord Jesus Christ, the Father of glory, may give to you a spirit of wisdom and of revelation in the knowledge of Him. [18] *I* pray that the eyes of your heart may be enlightened, so that you will know what is the hope of His calling, what are the riches of the glory of His inheritance in the saints" (Ephesians 1:16-18). Do we pray to have a deeper relationship with God? When we study the scriptures, do we study with the goal of not just accumulating facts, but knowing **Him** better?

Not everyone will choose to know God. In 2 Thessalonians 1:8-9, the apostle Paul warned that Jesus would come "dealing out retribution to those who do not know God and to those who do not obey the gospel of our Lord Jesus. [9] These will pay the penalty of eternal destruction, away from the presence of the Lord and from the glory of His power." There is no reason for not knowing God. He wants us to know Him so much that He has revealed Himself to us. God is so good to know.

❧LESSON 11❧

GROWING IN
GRACE AND KNOWLEDGE
Class Preparation

◊ **Things to Do:**

I.   Find a verse that tells us about God.

II.   Read Ephesians 4:14-15.

  A. Christians are no longer to act like

____

  B. What would toss them around?

  C. What would carry them about?

  D. Instead, speaking the truth in love, we are to do what?

III.   Read 2 Peter 3:18. What are we to grow in?

IV.   Read Titus 2:11-14. How are we to live?

V.   Read 2 Timothy 2:1. What are we to be strong in?

VI.   Read Hebrews 12:28. How are we to serve God?

Question for Class Discussion. Imagine yourself in 20 years. Will you grow in your faith between now and then? How will you do it?

⁋LESSON 11⁋

GROWING IN GRACE AND KNOWLEDGE
Class Reading

It is very easy to go through life either skipping along, quite satisfied, or being so burdened down with guilt that we continue to be stuck in a spiritual rut. But look how the apostle Peter talks about growth. He had just warned not to be led away by false teachers, " But grow in the grace and knowledge of our Lord and Savior Jesus Christ. To Him be the glory, both now and to the day of eternity. Amen" (2 Peter 3:18). Look at what we are to grow in: "The grace and knowledge of our Lord and Savior Jesus Christ."

Growing in the grace and knowledge of Jesus is developing our relationship with Him so that we become more and more like Him. Peter describes Jesus here as both our Lord and our Savior. We must continue to grow in our submission to Jesus as Lord and in our worship of Him as Savior. It reminds us that our goal in this study is to become closer to God more and more every day as we walk in His footsteps. By that we will grow in His grace and knowledge.

Ephesians 4:13-15 explains how to grow up in Christ in the context of church unity. "Until we all attain to the unity of the faith, and of the knowledge of the Son of God, to a mature man, to the measure of the stature which belongs to the fullness of Christ. [14] As a result, we are no longer to be children, tossed here and there by waves and carried about by every wind of doctrine, by the trickery of men, by craftiness in deceitful scheming; [15]but speaking the truth in love, we are to grow up in all aspects into Him who is the head, even Christ." We are not to be like children that have no stability. Spiritual maturity allows us to speak the truth to one another with love, so that we can all grow in maturity. That is what God wants of us.

The word of God is an integral part of our growth. Peter says, "Like newborn babies, long for the pure milk of the word, so that by it you may grow in respect to salvation" (1 Peter 2:2). We've all seen babies crave milk. That is how we must long for God's word, so that we might grow. But what if we do not crave it like we should? Then perhaps we have not focused our study on its proper purpose. We don't approach the word merely as a duty to be performed. We must realize that we cannot know God without knowing His word, and the purpose of our study is to know God.

As we seek spiritual growth, we should ask God for wisdom concerning our maturity. God desires for us to grow spiritually, and He has given us all we need to experience spiritual growth, but we must desire it and work towards it. We can ask God to increase our faith and knowledge of Him. Look at how the apostle Paul prayed for those in Colossae. "For this reason also, since the day we heard of it, we have not ceased to pray for you and to ask that you may be filled with the knowledge of His will in all spiritual wisdom and understanding, [10] so that you will walk in a manner worthy of the Lord, to please Him in all respects, bearing fruit in every good work and increasing in the knowledge of God" (Colossians 1:9-10). We can pray this prayer for ourselves and for others.

❧ LESSON 12 ❧
MAKING GOD OUR LIFE'S DEVOTION
Class Preparation

◊ **Things to Do:**

I. Write a verse about God.

II. Read Ecclesiastes 12:1, 13-14.

   A. In Ecclesiastes 12:1, what did Solomon say we should do in the days of our youth?

   B. In Ecclesiastes 12:13-14, what did Solomon say was the "conclusion of the whole matter"?

III. Read Matthew 6:33. What two things are we to seek first in our lives?

IV. Read Psalms 23:6

   A. What will follow David all his life?

   B. Where will he dwell?

   C. For how long?

Question for Class Discussion. God's way is the best way to live our lives. Following God will cause us to be good neighbors. Following God will make us kind and generous friends. God's way will make us strong and faithful church members. Following God will make families strong. Is there anything that we could name where God's way is not the best way?

❧ LESSON 12 ❧

MAKING GOD OUR LIFE'S DEVOTION
Self-Evaluation

Perhaps we have been in bible class and preaching all our lives, but do we think of how it impacts our lives to know about God? What a treasure it is to have this way of life that so many do not have. We need to realize that God's way of life is the best way. Look at people around you in church. Their lives are blessed. Thank God for this blessing. And as we thank Him, we pray to make a life-long commitment to Him, to love Him and serve Him all our lives. It is the way to have a good life.

Directions: You don't have to write these answers. Just think carefully about them.

Do I strive to

Draw close to God?

Seek God with all my heart?

Believe in God and believe God?

Love God with all my heart?

Love God by loving others?

Love God by Obeying Him?

Live a godly life as a young person so that I can become a godly woman?

Learn to be the kind of wife that God would have me someday be?

Follow Jesus?

Grow in grace and knowledge in the Lord Jesus Christ?

Make God my life's devotion?

❧LESSON 12❧
MAKING GOD OUR
LIFE'S DEVOTION
Class Reading

Are we determined to commit to God in complete devotion to fulfilling His purpose for us? If we are, we are making the best decision that we could ever make. We are guaranteeing wonderful lives for ourselves.

Perhaps the scripture that first comes to mind when we think of total commitment to God is when Jesus said, "You shall love the Lord your God with all your heart, and with all your soul, and with all your mind. [38] This is the great and foremost commandment" (Matthew 22:37). Love the Lord with everything that we are. First and foremost, our commitment hinges on our love for God.

To love God with our whole being, we must exercise that love. We may not wake up every morning with our heart focused on the Lord, eager to do His will but rather may be so busy starting our day that He does not even cross our minds. But we can remedy that. Determine to pray a prayer of thanksgiving every morning before we rise. When the alarm rings, pray, "Thank you, Lord, for this day. Today I seek to do Your will." Lay your Bible where you will see it so you won't forget. Leave a note on your refrigerator. We *must* make Him our focus. And when we do, it will be a great blessing to us.

No one is reading these words and saying, "Well, this is easy—no problem." No, to put God's will before our own is a life-long effort. Some days are harder than others: selfish days, proudful days, lustful days. Those are hard, but God is here, wanting us, pursuing us, seeking us, helping us, and forgiving us. Some days were hard even for Jesus, were they not?

We must understand that this commitment we make to God is not just one time when we accept Christ as our Savior and are baptized into Him. It is a daily, hourly, sometimes moment-by-moment dedication, that brings a lifetime of joy that can only be experienced through a close relationship with God.

Look down the pathway of your life. When the apostle Paul was near death he wrote, "For I am now ready to be offered, and the time of my departure is at hand. I have fought a good fight, I have finished the course, I have kept the faith" (2 Timothy 4:6-7). That is what we want to be able to say.

In a very touching farewell meeting with the Ephesian elders he said to them, "However, I consider my life worth nothing to me; my only aim is to finish the race and complete the task the Lord Jesus has given me—the task of testifying to the good news of God's grace" (Acts 20:24 NIV).

With these words, the Holy Spirit through Paul exhorts *us* to live in devotion to God: "Let us not lose heart in doing good, for in due time we will reap if we do not grow weary" (Galatians 6:9). How many have you known that started, but did not finish, who grew weary and gave up? Consider these other exhortations.

Hebrews 12:2-3: "Fixing our eyes on Jesus, the author and perfecter of faith, who for the joy set before Him endured the cross, despising the shame, and has sat down at the right hand of the throne of God.[3] For consider Him who has endured such hostility by sinners against Himself, so that you will not grow weary and lose heart." Think of what Jesus did for us and devote our life to Him.

Philippians 3:12, 14: "Not that I have already obtained it or have already become perfect, but I press on so that I may lay hold of that for which also was laid hold of by Christ Jesus… [14] I press on toward the goal for the prize of the upward call of God in Christ Jesus." Press on in devotion to God.

In our wedding ceremony, we make a promise to never give up: "Till death do us part." Make that same commitment, that same vow, to God: "I will never give up on You. I will be faithful unto death." Every morning, make the commitment, "I will devote today to Your service. I will live for You today." Then, when we reach the end of our life's journey, we can say, "I have fought a good fight, I have finished the course, I have kept the faith."

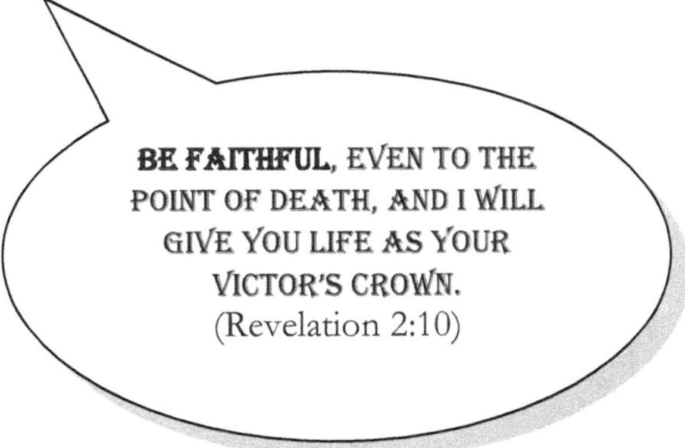

☙ LESSON 13 ❧

LIVING WITH GOD FOREVER
Class Preparation

◊ Things to Do:

    I.   Write a passage that describes God.

   II.   Read 1 John 2:28
  III.   Read Revelation 21:1-7
  IV.   Read Philippians 1:21-23
   V.   Read 1 Thessalonians 4:13-18
  VI.   Read 1 Corinthians 15:20-28.
VII.   Name an encouraging hymn about heaven. Read some of the lyrics in class.

Question for Class Discussion: It is hard for young people to think about dying without fear. But we can have great comfort in knowing that Jesus has prepared a wonderful place, and that He is waiting to welcome us home. What are some good things that will be in heaven? What are some bad things that won't be there? Will there be love in heaven? Will there be evil and hate? Any fear? Sickness? Dying? Joy? Think of more.

❧ LESSON 13 ❧

LIVE WITH GOD FOREVER
Class Reading

No class on drawing near to God could neglect the time when we will be in his actual presence like we can't be on earth. I'm sure that none of us want to die today, but we should always be ready to die. And we can realize that when we do, there will be something wonderful, more wonderful than we can even imagine, waiting for us.

Have you ever been truly homesick? When my husband was in the Marines, he had to be away from home for two full years. How deep was that pain of yearning to see his mama, daddy, and family. When the day finally arrived to go home, his daddy met him at the Nashville airport. As he got off the plane, he spotted him waiting in the door. There is no telling how long his daddy had been standing in that door, waiting to welcome his son home.

Is that not how it is going to be when we go home to the Father? If we die before the Lord returns, our spirits are taken to Paradise, the same place that Jesus went after His death, where the righteous are comforted (Luke 16:19-31). After the Lord returns, and after the resurrection and judgment, Jesus will take the saved home to the Father, all described in 1 Thessalonians 4:13-17.

We are longing for the day that the Lord will welcome us into our eternal home. In Colossians 3:1-2, Paul urges, "Therefore if you have been raised up with Christ, keep seeking the things above, where Christ is, seated at the right hand of God. [2] Set your mind on the things above, not on the things that are on earth." Let us heed the exhortation. "Keep seeking the things above" as we set our minds on things above. We are bound for the promised land!

And just as Jesus prepared the disciples for *His* leaving, He prepares us for *our* leaving. Paul assures us that when our body is torn down (death), we have another one from God, eternal in the heavens (2 Corinthians 5:1). In the eighth verse, Paul says, "We are of good courage, I say, and prefer rather to be absent from the body and to be at home with the Lord." Paul would rather be at home with the Lord than in his burdened, dying body. Paul believes that the glory of his eternal life will far outweigh the suffering of earthly life, and that is what we also should believe.

Then Paul condenses his life's goals into one single thing: to please Christ. "Therefore we also have as our ambition, whether at home or absent, to be pleasing to Him. [10] For we must all appear before the judgment seat of Christ, so that each one may be recompensed for his deeds in the body, according to what he has done, whether good or bad" (2 Corinthians 5:9-10). Whether here in difficult earthly life, or at home with Christ in glorious eternity, he wants to please Christ. That is Paul's ultimate purpose, and it is ours as well. Let us please Christ so that we can go home to the Father. Let us go home.

LIVE WITH GOD FOREVER
Hymn Lyrics

When We All Get to Heaven

1 Sing the wondrous love of Jesus,
Sing His mercy and His grace;
In the mansions bright and blessed
He'll prepare for us a place.

Refrain:

When we all get to heaven,
what a day of rejoicing that will be!
When we all see Jesus,
we'll sing and shout the victory!

2 While we walk the pilgrim pathway
Clouds will overspread the sky;
But when trav'ling days are over
Not a shadow, not a sigh. [Refrain]

3 Let us then be true and faithful,
Trusting, serving ev'ry day;
Just one glimpse of Him in glory
Will the toils of life repay. [Refrain]

4 Onward to the prize before us!
Soon His beauty we'll behold;
Soon the pearly gates will open–
We shall tread the streets of gold. [Refrain]

(Activities to be used with any lesson)

All About God

Crossword Clues

Across

2. We hold Him in ___.
4. Number of true Gods
5. Always true to Himself.
7. Compassionate
9. Without evil
11. Lasts forever
14. Awareness, comprehension

Down

1. Separate, unique
3. Uses great judgment
6. Opposite of false
8. Moral and upright
10. Willing to wait
12. Exists, actual
13. Affectionate and caring

Sing Praises

Fill in the blanks using the code on the next page.

1. __ __ __   __ __   __ __
   7 15 4   9 19   19 15

   __ __ __ __.
   7 15 15 4

2. __ __ __   __ __ __ __ __
   8 15 23   7 18 5 1 20

   __ __ __ __   __ __ __.
   20 8 15 21   1 18 20

3. __ __ __ __ __ __   __ __ __
   16 18 1 9 19 5   8 9 13

   __ __ __ __ __ __   __ __ __
   16 18 1 9 19 5   8 9 13

4. __ __ __ __   __ __ __ __
   8 15 12 25   8 15 12 25

   __ __ __ __
   8 15 12 25

Code

A	B	C	D	E	F	G	H	I	J
1	2	3	4	5	6	7	8	9	10
K	L	M	N	O	P	Q	R	S	T
11	12	13	14	15	16	17	18	19	20
U	V	W	X	Y	Z				
21	22	23	24	25	26				

GOD IS...

Directions: Unscramble these words that describe God.

1. fetinnii   ______________

2. odog   ______________

3. seiw   ______________

4. thiafiuf   ______________

5. criflume   ______________

6. veol   ______________

7. yolh   ______________

8. sourthige   ______________

9. tinetap   ______________

10. sourilog   ______________

www.ingramcontent.com/pod-product-compliance
Lightning Source LLC
Chambersburg PA
CBHW050801160726
48004CB00002B/649